A Dedicated Prayer Lifestyle: Simple Tips To Effective Prayer Lifestyle

Johannes Tefo

Published by Johannes Tefo, 2024.

Also by Johannes Tefo

Family spiritual Warfare Books
Generational Curses And Spiritual Warfare: Spiritual Strategies
& Principles Of Victory Against Evil Strongholds
Youth's Guide To Spiritual Warfare
A Women's Guide To Spiritual Warfare

Standalone
Deliver Your Soul From Evil
Overcoming Spirit Of Stagnation
The 24: Prophetic Word For This Season 2024 And Beyond
Michael For Warfare
Territorial Spirits: Overcome Evil Strongholds in Your Life And
Take Over Your Community With Strategic Warfare And Winning Prayers
Prayers Against Suicide Spirit
Spiritual Warfare When Enough is Enough
Identity In Christ
Prayers Against Satanic Networks

The Workplace You Need: Spiritual Warfare Prayers That Silence Evil Powers At Your Workplace.

Deliverance From Mind Control: Be Free And Delivered From Every Marine Demons Of Mind Control

Times Getting Hard: Scriptures Of Comfort For Hard Days

Battle In The Sea: How To Tackle Spiritual Warfare And Win The Battle

Freedom: Deliverance Of Souls From Captivity

A Dedicated Prayer Lifestyle: Simple Tips To Effective Prayer Lifestyle

Redefined By Fire: Unleashing The Power Of The Holy Spirit Within.

Table of Contents

1. Set a Regular Prayer Time

Establish a specific time each day dedicated to prayer. Consistency builds discipline and strengthens your connection with God. When a person is connected to God in spirit, soul, and body, he or she becomes a different person from the rest. It is a life of holiness and separation that makes men and women extraordinary. An individual can only think up to a certain point or limit, then after that, it is the grace of the wisdom of the Living God that takes over. Prayer is a necessity in all aspects of life.

You can pray at any time but when you have a prayer time, it makes life a little bit easier. And if you stick to it with all passion and dedication, the fire in you will be burning like a torch. When fire is in you, it is no longer you but God's mighty spirit that manifests itself in different situations. A life led by the spirit of God is a life worth living at any day and time.

The Spirit of Christ is a spirit of the solution to situations. When we press in, in the secret place of prayer, we come out looking like Christ transfigured by light, or Moses overshadowed by the light of the glory of God. A man is a spirit, soul, and body, from a spiritual perspective, when you are looking at someone who has mastered a serious prayer lifestyle, you are looking at the covering of a beam of light.

Normally, you can start small. Even a 5 minutes prayer matters to God. You can always develop into lengthy prayers as the spirit of God inspires you. The spirit of might inspire and give you strength to go beyond.

When we wake up in the morning, when it is a new beautiful day, we are to worship and pray. We pray a thanksgiving prayer unto the Father of all souls for keeping us. Gratitude prayers can change our lives.

Again, when we sleep, it is also a call for prayer. We petition for the mercy of God to keep us and protect us against all harm. There are arrows of evil that are assigned at us, day and night, this arrows are strengthened at night because of the power of darkness. Darkness is a spirit. light is a spirit.

A call to a prayer time will keep us focused on the things of the kingdom. While temptations will always be there, tests, trials, and tribulations, a life of prayer will keep us strong in stormy times.

How to Set a Regular Time for Prayer

Finding a regular time for prayer can bring so much peace and joy into your life. It's like having a daily chat with your best friend—God. Here are some easy steps to help you set a regular prayer time:

1. **Pick a Time That Works for You**
   - **Morning**: Right after you wake up, spend a few minutes thanking God for the new day.
   - **Evening**: Before going to bed, reflect on your day and pray for a restful night.
   - **Midday**: Take a break during lunch to pray for strength for the rest of the day.
2. **Start Small**
   - Begin with 5-10 minutes. You can always extend the time as you get used to it. The important thing is to start.

3. **Set a Reminder**
    - Use your phone or a clock to set an alarm to remind you of your prayer time. This helps you remember and keeps you on track.

4. **Create a Prayer Space**
    - Find a quiet and comfortable place where you can pray without interruptions. It could be a corner of your room, a chair by the window, or even a spot in your garden.

5. **Use a Prayer Journal**
    - Write down your prayers and any thoughts you have. This helps you focus and also lets you look back and see how God has answered your prayers.

6. **Follow a Routine**
    - Start with a simple routine:
        - **Thanksgiving**: Thank God for the blessings in your life.
        - **Requests**: Pray for your needs and the needs of others.
        - **Listening**: Spend a moment in silence, listening for God's voice.

7. **Stay Flexible**
    - Life can be busy and plans can change. If you miss a prayer time, don't worry. Just pick it up again the next day. God understands.

8. **Pray with Others**
    - Sometimes praying with a friend or family member can be encouraging. You can share your prayer time once a week or whenever it's

possible.

9. **Stay Encouraged**
    ◦ Remember that prayer is a journey. Every little step you take brings you closer to God. Celebrate the progress you make, no matter how small it seems.

Friend, making time for prayer is a beautiful way to grow in your faith and feel God's presence in your daily life. Take it one day at a time, and know that every prayer matters.

This guide is designed to be easy to follow and to encourage regular prayer habits simply and practically.

2. Create a Prayer List

Keep a list of people, situations, and issues to pray for. This helps you stay organized and ensures that you cover all your prayer concerns regularly.

Yes, a prayer list is necessary at times. If you are someone who has a heart for the nations, or you receive prophetic dreams and visions concerning nations, a prayer journal should be your next buddy. It's where you will write what the spirit of the Lord shows you and tells you. And at times you will be writing prayer lists, symbols in dreams, visions and prophetic impressions, and more.

Back in the days' believers used to do spiritual mapping to take down strongmen of a certain region. They will study the people, the atmosphere, and the patterns they see through the language, songs, culture, and traditions.

And this is where serious prayer lists are developed to dismantle the powers of darkness ruling a certain place. Prophetic believers always have to have prayer lists, prayer journals, etc. Likewise, the student of the Bible, studies to show himself or herself approved as a workman.

As most of us come from a lineage of idol worship and rebellion to the will of God, we ought to make notes about the spiritual patterns we see in our families. Dreams and visions are very important as they hold the pathway of the mysteries of our lives.

I strongly believe that every person on this earth, a believer or non-believer, through their dreams, can know the purpose of God on this earth. God through dreams talked to believers and non-believers alike. If He conversed with Nebuchadnezzar and other pagan kings, He would also reach His children through any means.

Hold on to your prayer lists. Keep reading the Word of God and scriptures that speak volumes to your heart, keep them, meditate on them, and pray for them. Pray for the nations, pray for your family, friends, and community, and for the will of God to overtake any will of men on this planet.

Believe the Holy Father in the name of Jesus Christ. There are many misleading teachings about the name of Jesus. We know the name holds power in heaven, on earth, and earth below as someone who has seen the underworld, the most feared name in all universe is the name of Jesus Christ. It is the name of power.

Daily Prayer List for Strength and Encouragement

As you walk through this season of your life, remember that you are never alone. Prayer is your direct line to God, and through it, you can find peace, strength, and guidance. Here's a prayer list to inspire and uplift you. Take a moment each day to connect with God, and let His love fill your heart.

1. **Morning Gratitude**
    - **Scripture**: "Give thanks to the Lord, for He is good; His love endures forever." – Psalm 107:1
    - **Prayer**: Heavenly Father, thank You for this new day. Thank You for the breath in my lungs and the opportunities that lie ahead. Help me to see Your blessings in every moment and to start my day with a grateful heart.
2. **Strength for the Day**

- **Scripture**: "I can do all things through Christ who strengthens me." – Philippians 4:13
- **Prayer**: Lord, I ask for Your strength to face the challenges of today. Equip me with courage and perseverance. When I feel weak, remind me that Your power is made perfect in my weakness.

3. **Guidance and Wisdom**
   - **Scripture**: "Trust in the Lord with all your heart and lean not on your own understanding; in all your ways submit to Him, and He will make your paths straight." – Proverbs 3:5-6
   - **Prayer**: Father, I seek Your wisdom in every decision I make today. Guide my steps and enlighten my mind. Help me to trust in Your plan and to rely on Your understanding, not my own.

4. **Peace and Calm**
   - **Scripture**: "Do not be anxious about anything, but in every situation, by prayer and petition, with thanksgiving, present your requests to God. And the peace of God, which transcends all understanding, will guard your hearts and your minds in Christ Jesus." – Philippians 4:6-7
   - **Prayer**: Lord, calm my anxious heart. Replace my worries with Your peace. Help me to surrender my fears to You and to rest in the

knowledge that You are in control.

5. Forgiveness and Grace

- **Scripture**: "Be kind and compassionate to one another, forgiving each other, just as in Christ God forgave you." – Ephesians 4:32
- **Prayer**: Jesus, help me to forgive others as You have forgiven me. Fill my heart with compassion and grace. Teach me to let go of grudges and to love others as You love me.

1. Strengthening Relationships

- **Scripture**: "A friend loves at all times, and a brother is born for a time of adversity." – Proverbs 17:17
- **Prayer**: Lord, bless my relationships with family and friends. Give me the patience, understanding, and love needed to nurture these bonds. Help me to be a source of support and encouragement to those around me.

1. Nighttime Reflection

- **Scripture**: "In peace I will lie down and sleep, for You alone, Lord, make me dwell in safety." – Psalm 4:8
- **Prayer**: Father, as I close my eyes tonight, I reflect on Your goodness throughout the day. Thank You for Your protection and provision. Grant me restful sleep and fill my dreams with Your presence.

3. Study the Bible

Immerse yourself in God's Word. Understanding the Scriptures enhances your prayers, aligning them with God's will.

It is vital to elevate your prayer lifestyle when trouble mounts up. If you used to pray for 5 minutes, double it up. The student of the bible is a person of prayer inspired and moved by the Word of God. David inspired himself in the Lord and continued with the journey of faith even at point it seemed impossible.

Psalm 119:24 Thy testimonies also are my delight and my counsellors.

The law of the Lord became his counselor. God is the rewarder of those who are faithful in His Word, He rewards them for their faith, dedication, and their zealousness. Jesus Christ was zealous for the house of God—the man of righteousness. Righteous men hate even the stain of sin. They live a life pleasing to God.

Psalm 69:9 For the zeal of thine house hath eaten me up; and the reproaches of them
that reproached thee are fallen upon me.

The students of the bible have a zeal for the kingdom of God upon the earth. they have a zeal for the mind and the will of God. They are God pleasers rather than men-pleasers.

8 It is better to trust in the LORD than to put confidence in man.
9 It is better to trust in the LORD than to put confidence in princes.
Psalm 118:8-9.

The Lord God the Holy Father in the name of Jesus Christ is who we look for, those in authority may help us here and there, but they have their limit, God is limitless. If you want to go far in life, trust the Lord God at all times.

In Africa and most parts of the world, we have made religious men to be demi-gods or junior gods to the point where we no longer look up to Jesus Christ, who is the author and the finisher of our faith. Apostles, prophets, bishops, and pastors are drawing congregants to themselves instead of pointing them to their maker, He who made the heavens and the earth.

Keep your faith pure, walk in the truth of the common faith, and work out your salvation in the name of the Lord. With all kinds of prayers, we should seek the face of the Lord and pray according to the will and the mind of the Holy Spirit.

Praying in the Holy Ghost will strengthen our faith. The weak man is strengthened when we stir ourselves up in the Holy faith mentioned by Jude.

3 Beloved, when I gave all diligence to write unto you of the common

mon

salvation, it was needful for me to write unto you, and exhort you that ye should

earnestly contend for the faith which was once delivered unto the saints.

Jude 1:3.

20 But ye, beloved, building up yourselves on your most holy faith, praying

in the Holy Ghost,

21 Keep yourselves in the love of God, looking for the mercy of our Lord

Jesus Christ unto eternal life.

These two scriptures exhorts us to earnestly contend for the faith which was once delivered unto the saints. The common salvation of the undiluted kingdom of God. The gospel does not please men but convicts them to follow Christ in righteousness and holiness. In all readiness of peace and meekness.

At the end of the race, it is the holy faith that will keep us. Faith is a forever trend; it does not come out of fashion. God will honor faith. He the rewards faith. And faith is the result of the Word of God.

It is written;

8 But what saith it? The word is nigh thee, even in thy mouth, and in thy

heart: that is, the word of faith, which we preach;

9 That if thou shalt confess with thy mouth the Lord Jesus, and shalt believe

in thine heart that God hath raised him from the dead, thou shalt be saved.

10 For with the heart man believeth unto righteousness; and with the mouth

confession is made unto salvation.

11 For the scripture saith, Whosoever believeth on him shall not be ashamed.

Romans 10:8-11.

Romans 10:17 So then faith cometh by hearing, and hearing by the word of God.

Total deliverance comes when we immerse ourselves in the Word and maintains of our deliverance also comes when the Word is in us. It is critical and highly important to be a student of the bible. Faith is quickened by the Word.

Hear the Word, and live.

John 6:63 It is the spirit that quickeneth; the flesh profiteth nothing: the words that I

speak unto you, they are spirit, and they are life.

Study prayer patterns of the bible.

Sincere prayers that come from the heart of a believer have no formula. The Holy Spirit in us lead us to prayer the prayer that aligns with the will of God. Any prayer that is outside the will of God will surely be disappointed. However, there are a few prayers that we can learn and model in the bible.

Jesus Christ taught His disciples how to pray. John the Baptist also taught his disciples to pray. In the old covenant, God taught Moses the Aaronic priesthood blessing prayer (Number 6:24).

Right prayers will always be answered by the righteous Father. The author and the finisher of our faith is Jesus Christ. By all means, we ought to follow the example Jesus Christ set. Paul says *"Follow me as I follow Christ"*.

Back in the day, I copied all the prayers men and women of God prayed in the bible, and diligently studied them, and how they were answered. And I concluded that heartfelt prayers will never be despised. Above that, prayer that has its stand on the Word were always answered.

How to Be a Student of the Bible

Studying the Bible is a wonderful way to grow closer to God and understand His plans for your life. Here are some simple steps to help you become a dedicated student of the Bible:

1. **Choose a Regular Time**
   - Pick a time each day to read the Bible. It could

be in the morning, during lunch, or before bed. Find a time that works best for you and stick to it.

2. **Find a Quiet Place**
   - Choose a spot where you can read without distractions. It might be a cozy chair, a corner of your room, or even a park bench.

3. **Use a Bible You Understand**
   - Make sure you have a Bible translation that is easy to read. Versions like the New International Version (NIV) or the New Living Translation (NLT) are great choices.

4. **Start with a Plan**
   - Follow a reading plan to guide your study. You can find plans that cover specific topics, books of the Bible, or the entire Bible in a year. Many Bibles and websites offer these plans.

5. **Take Notes**
   - Keep a notebook or journal to write down your thoughts, questions, and insights. This helps you remember what you've learned and see your growth over time.

6. **Pray for Understanding**
   - Before you start reading, pray and ask God to help you understand His Word. Ask Him to open your heart and mind to His teachings.

7. **Read Small Sections**
   - Start with small passages or a few verses each day. Don't rush through it. Take your time to understand and reflect on what you read.

8. **Reflect and Apply**
    - Think about how the passage applies to your life. Ask yourself questions like:
        - What is God teaching me in this verse?
        - How can I apply this lesson to my daily life?
        - Is there something I need to change based on what I've read?

1. **Join a Study Group**
    - Studying the Bible with others can be very helpful. Join a Bible study group at your church or with friends. Sharing insights and discussing passages together can deepen your understanding.
2. **Use Helpful Resources**
    - Use study aids like commentaries, Bible dictionaries, and online resources to gain more insight. These tools can help explain difficult passages and provide historical context.
3. **Memorize Verses**
    - Try to memorize key verses that speak to you. This helps you keep God's Word in your heart and mind, especially during challenging times.
4. **Stay Consistent**
    - Consistency is key. Even if you can only read for a few minutes each day, make it a habit.

Over time, you'll see your knowledge and faith grow.

Friend, becoming a student of the Bible is a lifelong journey. Take it one step at a time, and enjoy discovering the depths of God's love and wisdom. Remember, God is always with you, guiding and teaching you through His Word

4. Pray with Faith

Believe in the power of prayer and trust that God hears and answers. Approach prayer with confidence, knowing that God is faithful.

I want to share with you the incredible power of praying in faith. When we pray, we are not just speaking words into the air; we are communicating directly with our loving Heavenly Father. Praying in faith means trusting that God hears us and believing that He will answer our prayers according to His perfect will. It is a beautiful act of surrender and hope, knowing that our concerns and desires are in the hands of the One who loves us most.

One of the most comforting aspects of praying in faith is knowing that God is always listening. Psalm 34:17 assures us, "The righteous cry out, and the Lord hears them; He delivers them from all their troubles." This verse reminds us that our cries do not go unnoticed. God hears every whisper, every plea, and every shout of our hearts. Even when it feels like our prayers are not being answered immediately, we can hold onto the promise that God is attentive and working in ways we may not yet see.

Praying in faith also means believing in God's goodness and His desire to bless us. Psalm 37:4 encourages us to "Take delight in the Lord, and He will give you the desires of your heart." When we align our hearts with God's, our desires start to reflect His will. This doesn't mean we always get what we want, but it does mean that God's plans for us are always for our good, even if they differ from our own.

Faith-filled prayer is grounded in hope. Psalm 42:11 says, "Why, my soul, are you downcast? Why so disturbed within me? Put your hope in God, for I will yet praise Him, my Savior and my God." This verse speaks to those moments when we feel discouraged or overwhelmed. It is a call to lift our eyes to God and place our hope in Him. When we pray with hope, we are choosing to trust that God's promises are true and that He is faithful to fulfill them.

One of the most powerful examples of praying in faith comes from Jesus Himself. In Mark 11:24, Jesus tells His disciples, "Therefore I tell you, whatever you ask for in prayer, believe that you have received it, and it will be yours." Jesus encourages us to pray with the expectation that God will answer. This doesn't mean we will always receive exactly what we ask for, but it means we should pray with the confidence that God's answer will be what is best for us.

Praying in faith also involves waiting on God's timing. Psalm 27:14 advises us, "Wait for the Lord; be strong and take heart and wait for the Lord." Patience is often a challenging part of faith, but it is essential. God's timing is perfect, and His delays are not denials. During the waiting period, God is often working in our hearts, growing our faith, and preparing us for the blessings to come.

In moments of doubt, it is helpful to remember the faithfulness of God in the past. Psalm 77:11-12 encourages us to recall God's deeds: "I will remember the deeds of the Lord; yes, I will remember your miracles of long ago. I will consider all your works and meditate on all your mighty deeds." Reflecting on how God has answered prayers before can bolster our faith and renew our hope.

[Friend's Name], as you continue to lift your prayers to God, do so with a heart full of faith and hope. Trust that He hears you, loves you, and is working all things together for your good. Stand firm in the promises of His Word, and let the Psalms remind you of His faithfulness and love. Your prayers matter, and your faith moves mountains. Keep praying, believing, and hoping for our amazing God.

Practical Ways to Pray in Faith

Praying in faith is a powerful way to connect with God and trust in His plans for our lives. Here are some practical steps to help you pray with confidence and faith:

1. **Start with Thanksgiving**
   - Begin your prayer by thanking God for His blessings. Gratitude helps you focus on God's goodness and sets a positive tone for your prayer.
   - **Example**: "Heavenly Father, thank You for Your love and for the blessings You have given me. Thank You for being with me every day."

2. **Speak God's Promises**
   - Use Scripture in your prayers to remind yourself of God's promises. This strengthens your faith and aligns your prayers with God's Word.
   - **Example**: "Lord, Your Word says that You hear the cries of the righteous (Psalm 34:17). I trust that You are listening to my prayers and will answer them according to Your will."

3. **Pray Specifically**

- Be specific about your needs and desires. When you pray with clear requests, it helps you to recognize God's answers and gives you a clear focus in your prayers.
- **Example**: "Father, I pray for healing for my friend who is sick. Please give them strength and restore their health."

4. **Believe and Trust**
    - As you pray, believe that God is capable of answering your prayers and trust in His timing and methods.
    - **Example**: "Lord, I believe that You can do all things. I trust that You know what is best for me and that You will answer my prayers in Your perfect timing."

5. **Express Your Faith**
    - Speak words of faith during your prayers. Declare your trust in God and your belief in His power.
    - **Example**: "God, I know that nothing is impossible for You. I trust that You are working all things together for my good (Romans 8:28)."

6. **Listen and Reflect**
    - Take time to be still and listen for God's voice. Reflect on what He might be saying to you through your prayers and the Scriptures.
    - **Example**: "Lord, I am here, waiting and listening for Your guidance. Speak to my heart

and show me Your will."

7. **Release Your Worries**
    ◦ Give your worries and fears to God. Trust that He is in control and will take care of your needs.
    ◦ **Example**: "Father, I release my anxieties to You. I know that You care for me and will provide for all my needs (1 Peter 5:7)."

8. **Stay Persistent**
    ◦ Keep praying even when you don't see immediate answers. Persistence in prayer shows your trust in God's faithfulness.
    ◦ **Example**: "God, I will continue to pray and trust in You, even when I don't see the answers right away. I know that You are faithful and will answer in Your time."

9. **End with Praise**
    ◦ Finish your prayer by praising God for His goodness and faithfulness. Praise reinforces your trust and faith in Him.
    ◦ **Example**: "Lord, I praise You for Your goodness and faithfulness. Thank You for hearing my prayers and for the answers that are on their way."

Praying in faith is about trusting God fully and believing that He is able and willing to act on your behalf. It's about having confidence in His promises and resting in His love. Remember, [Friend's Name], that God delights in your prayers and is always ready to respond with His perfect wisdom and timing.

5. Be Persistent

Don't give up on your prayers, even if answers seem delayed. Persistence in prayer demonstrates faith and commitment.

There is a profound strength and beauty in being persistent in prayer. It's a practice that not only deepens our relationship with God but also shapes our character and faith. Persisting in prayer means continuing to pray even when answers seem delayed, when the circumstances look unchanged, and when doubts creep in. It's about having faith that God is listening, that He cares and that He will act in His perfect timing.

One of the most powerful examples of persistence in prayer comes from Jesus Himself. In Luke 18:1-8, Jesus tells the parable of the persistent widow. This widow kept coming to an unjust judge, pleading for justice. Despite his reluctance, the judge eventually granted her request because of her persistence. Jesus uses this story to teach us about the importance of never giving up in prayer. He says, "And will not God bring about justice for His chosen ones, who cry out to Him day and night? Will He keep putting them off? I tell you, He will see that they get justice, and quickly" (Luke 18:7-8). This parable reassures us that if an unjust judge can be moved by persistence, how much more will our loving and just God respond to our persistent prayers?

Persistence in prayer is an act of faith. It demonstrates that we trust God's character and His promises. When we continue to pray, we are essentially saying, "Lord, I believe You are good. I believe You are faithful. I believe You have a plan, even if I don't understand it right now." This unwavering commitment to prayer strengthens our faith and brings us closer to God. It allows us to experience His peace, even in uncertainty.

The Psalms are filled with expressions of persistent prayer. Psalm 40:1-3 beautifully captures the experience of waiting on the Lord: "I waited patiently for the Lord; He turned to me and heard my cry. He lifted me out of the slimy pit, out of the mud and mire; He set my feet on a rock and gave me a firm place to stand. He put a new song in my mouth, a hymn of praise to our God." This passage reminds us that God hears our cries and responds to our persistence. It may take time, but His response will come, lifting us out of our difficulties and setting us on a firm foundation.

Being persistent in prayer also means being honest with God about our struggles and doubts. Psalm 13 is a poignant example of this honesty: "How long, Lord? Will You forget me forever? How long will You hide Your face from me? How long must I wrestle with my thoughts and day after day have sorrow in my heart?" (Psalm 13:1-2). Yet, despite the anguish, the Psalmist ends with a declaration of trust: "But I trust in Your unfailing love; my heart rejoices in Your salvation. I will sing the Lord's praise, for He has been good to me" (Psalm 13:5-6). This shows us that persistence in prayer includes bringing our raw emotions to God, while also holding onto our trust in His goodness.

Persistence in prayer is not about wearing God down or trying to change His mind. It's about aligning our hearts with His, growing in our reliance on Him, and trusting that His ways are higher than ours. As we persist, we are transformed. Our perspectives shift, our faith deepens, and we begin to see our circumstances through the lens of God's eternal purpose.

Keep pressing on in your prayers. Know that every prayer, every tear, every moment spent in God's presence is not in vain. God hears you, He loves you, and He is at work in ways you cannot yet see. Let the words of Psalm 27:14 be your encouragement: "Wait for the Lord; be strong and take heart and wait for the Lord." Your persistence in prayer is a testament to your faith and trust in God, and it will bear fruit in His perfect time.

6. Pray in the Spirit

Allow the Holy Spirit to guide your prayers. Sometimes, praying in tongues or simply asking the Holy Spirit to lead can bring a deeper dimension to your prayer life.

The power prayers are those prayed in the Holy Ghost. The Holy Spirit of God teaches us how to pray. You will notice this when you have been praying for a long time. It will no longer be just you praying but the spirit in you will be interceding and making bold prayers you wouldn't normally do.

When you are praying in tongues, if you do not have the gift of interpreting tongues, you would surprise God to answer prayers you never thought you prayed. I remember at one point I was interceding and praying for the government of the nation of America unbeknown to me. Tongues are powerful. And can transform your life. However, we are not to abuse this precious gift of God, as many Pentecostal brothers and sisters do.

We pray with all kinds of prayers, meaning, when is time to sing, we sing, time to worship, we worship, and time for warfare, when engage in spiritual battle—the good fight of faith. We pray in spirit because our Father is a spirit being. Like us, we are spirit, soul, and body, it is vital to yearn for the life of spirit. spiritual life is above all.

And in the books of the life of spirit, it does not matter whether you are big or small, rich or poor, the spiritual life does not have a race or color. It is the life governed by the mighty Spirit of Jesus Christ. We follow Christ who conquered so that we can be conquerors too. However, it is not a walk in the part, it is a difficult journey of which we survive through the emblem of faith.

When we pray in the Holy Ghost, the man inside is strengthened. The spirit man is the most important being in us. It is He who connects us to the throne of God. Walking in the grace of power of God, allows us to deepen our walk with Him, and we are rest assured that where He is, so are we.

We are not waiting for to God to heaven but to propel His will through prayers to manifest while on Earth.

Heaven is a real place of the outer space dimension, however, Christ has brought heaven within us—and that is His Holy Spirit. we shall surely experience the greater glory of the Living God when we walk in spirit and pray in the Holy Ghost. We shall see wonders, signs, miracles, and the greater move of the Holy Spirit of these last days.

20 But ye, beloved, building up yourselves on your most holy faith,
praying
in the Holy Ghost,
21 Keep yourselves in the love of God, looking for the mercy of our
Lord
Jesus Christ unto eternal life.
Jude 1:20-21.

The most Holy faith is the common salvation that came through the Apostles and Prophets. It is clear that since many are falling away, deception will be at the peak of all things. The scripture says "Be ye not deceived". In this age, there are many strange Bibles, strange books, and strange teachings produced to lure many into the occult of deceptive spirits.

Many teaching comes from the marine world. Many anointing's come from the underworld. Men and women have tapped into forbidden kingdoms to acquire knowledge. Keep your faith pure.

How to Tap into the Supernatural

1. **Believe in Jesus**: Start by believing that Jesus is God's Son. He came to earth, died for our sins, and rose again. This faith is the first step to experiencing the supernatural.
2. **Read the Bible**: The Bible is God's word. Read it daily to understand God's will and to know His promises. The Bible is full of stories of God's supernatural power.
3. **Pray Regularly**: Talk to God through prayer. Thank Him, ask for His help, and share your thoughts and feelings. Prayer connects you to God's power.
4. **Obey God's Commands**: Follow what the Bible teaches. When you obey God, you are more open to His supernatural work in your life.

Praying in the Holy Ghost (Jude 1:20)

Jude 1:20 says, "But you, dear friends, by building yourselves up in your most holy faith and praying in the Holy Spirit."

Here is how you can pray in the Holy Ghost:

1. **Ask for the Holy Spirit**: Jesus promised that God would give the Holy Spirit to those who ask. Pray and ask God to fill you with the Holy Spirit.
2. **Pray with Sincerity**: Speak from your heart. The Holy Spirit helps us pray even when we don't have the right words.
3. **Pray with Faith**: Believe that God hears you and will answer according to His will. Trust that the Holy Spirit will guide your prayers.

4. **Pray in Tongues**: Some people are given the gift of speaking in tongues. This is a special language given by the Holy Spirit. If you feel led to, ask God for this gift.

5. **Stay Connected to God**: Keep a close relationship with God through regular prayer and reading the Bible. The more you connect with God, the more you will experience His supernatural power.

Remember, praying in the Holy Spirit is about letting God's Spirit guide you. Trust Him, and you will see amazing things happen in your life.

7. Use Scripture in Your Prayers

Incorporate Bible verses into your prayers. This not only strengthens your prayers but also affirms God's promises.

I liked how Elijah out of nowhere made a grand entrance into the palace of King Ahab and Jezebel. According to the law of Moses, if the nation of Israel leaves the true God and serves the strange God of whom their ancestors knew not, one of the plagues of many written in the law was no rain, that the heavens will be as iron bars.

Elijah stood on what was written in Deuteronomy 28 as the prophet of God. Basing your faith on scripture leads to victory in the court of the heavens. The court of heaven is a judicial government ruled by the laws of God. If you are not backed by His words, in most cases as believers, we stand disappointed.

Our enemy, Satan, is a man of law. If you break the law of God, it gives him the legal right to wreck your life to hell, to make your life miserable. It is by the grace of God and our advocate, Christ, that most time we are spared even when we are wrong. The grace saves. His Mercy endures forever.

I want you to learn about the power of praying God's word in this passage. When you are praying or worshipping the Word, you are canceling and erasing anything against you through the Word in the spirit realm. The word is power. In the spirit realm, the Word is the light. It is light that defeats darkness. We are the children of the light.

Isaiah 2:5 O house of Jacob, come ye, and let us walk in the light of the LORD.

Isaiah 2:5 says, "O house of Jacob, come ye, and let us walk in the light of the LORD." This verse invites us to live in the light of God's presence and guidance. Here are some simple and practical ways you can walk in the light of God daily:

Spend Time with God Every Day

Start each day by spending time with God through prayer and reading the Bible. Just as the sun gives light to the world, God's Word gives light to your life. Psalm 119:105 says, "Your word is a lamp to my feet and a light to my path." Let His Word guide your steps each day.

Follow Jesus' Example

Jesus is the light of the world. In John 8:12, Jesus says, "I am the light of the world. Whoever follows me will never walk in darkness but will have the light of life." Follow His teachings and example. Be kind, loving, and compassionate to others just as He was.

Stay Honest and True

Walking in the light means living a life of honesty and integrity. Ephesians 5:8-9 says, "For you were once darkness, but now you are light in the Lord. Live as children of light (for the fruit of the light consists in all goodness, righteousness, and truth)." Be truthful and do what is right, even when it's hard.

Shine Your Light

You are called to be a light to others. Matthew 5:14-16 says, "You are the light of the world. A town built on a hill cannot be hidden. Neither do people light a lamp and put it under a bowl. Instead, they put it on its stand, and it gives light to everyone in the house. In the same way, let your light shine before others, that they may see your good deeds and glorify your Father in heaven." Do good deeds and share God's love with others, so they can see His light through you.

Trust God in All Things

Walking in the light means trusting God, even when you don't understand everything. Proverbs 3:5-6 says, "Trust in the LORD with all your heart and lean not on your own understanding; in all your ways submit to him, and he will make your paths straight." Trust that God is guiding you and will lead you where you need to go.

Stay Connected with Other Believers

Being part of a community of believers helps you stay strong in your faith. Hebrews 10:24-25 says, "And let us consider how we may spur one another on toward love and good deeds, not giving up meeting together, as some are in the habit of doing but encouraging one another." Encourage and support each other in walking in the light of the Lord.

Reflect on God's Goodness

Regularly take time to reflect on God's goodness and faithfulness in your life. Psalm 92:1-2 says, "It is good to praise the LORD and make music to your name, O Most High, proclaiming your love in the morning and your faithfulness at night." Remembering His blessings helps you stay grateful and focused on His light.

By incorporating these simple practices into your daily life, you can walk in the light of the Lord and experience His guidance, peace, and joy. Let His light shine through you, bringing hope and love to those around you.

The practical way of praying His Word.

Praying God's Word is one of the most powerful ways to connect with Him and see real results in your life. When you pray using Scripture, you are aligning your heart and mind with God's truth and promises. This kind of prayer is powerful, profound, and transformative. Here's how you can adopt this practice and see the impact in your life.

The Power of Praying God's Word

When you pray the Scriptures, you are speaking God's own words back to Him. This aligns your prayers with His will and strengthens your faith. Hebrews 4:12 says, "For the word of God is alive and active. Sharper than any double-edged sword." By praying His Word, you are wielding a powerful tool that can change your circumstances and your heart.

Building Faith Through Scripture

Faith comes from hearing the Word of God (Romans 10:17). When you pray Scriptures, you remind yourself of God's promises and build your faith. For instance, if you are feeling anxious, pray Philippians 4:6-7: "Do not be anxious about anything, but in every situation, by prayer and petition, with thanksgiving, present your requests to God. And the peace of God, which transcends all understanding, will guard your hearts and your minds in Christ Jesus." This scripture helps you focus on God's peace rather than your worries.

God's Promises in Prayer

God's promises are powerful and unchanging. When you include His promises in your prayers, you remind yourself and declare your trust in His faithfulness. For example, if you need provision, pray Philippians 4:19: "And my God will meet all your needs according to the riches of his glory in Christ Jesus." This helps you rely on God's promise to provide for you, strengthening your trust in Him.

Praying for Strength and Guidance

In times of weakness or when you need guidance, praying Scriptures can provide the strength and direction you need. Isaiah 40:31 says, "But those who hope in the Lord will renew their strength. They will soar on wings like eagles; they will run and not grow weary, they will walk and not be faint." Praying this verse can give you the encouragement to keep going, knowing that God will renew your strength.

Overcoming Challenges with God's Word

Life is full of challenges, but God's Word gives you the power to overcome them. When you face temptation, pray 1 Corinthians 10:13: "No temptation has overtaken you except what is common to mankind. And God is faithful; he will not let you be tempted beyond what you can bear. But when you are tempted, he will also provide a way out so that you can endure it." This reminds you that God is with you and will help you overcome any challenge.

Experiencing Peace through Prayer

God's Word brings peace amid chaos. Praying scriptures like John 14:27 can fill you with peace: "Peace I leave with you; my peace I give you. I do not give to you as the world gives. Do not let your hearts be troubled and do not be afraid." This promise reassures you that God's peace is different and more profound than any peace the world offers.

Conclusion

Praying God's Word is a powerful practice that can transform your prayer life and deepen your relationship with God. It aligns your prayers with His will, builds your faith, and reminds you of His promises. By incorporating Scriptures into your prayers, you tap into the power of God's living and active Word. Start today by finding verses that speak to your needs and pray them with faith. You will see God's power and promises come alive in your life.

8. Join a Prayer Group

Praying with others can be incredibly powerful. Join a prayer group or start one with friends to support each other in prayer.

There are so many brothers and sisters on social media with a hunger for God. It is truly a blessing to be with believers who yearn for the fire of the Holy Spirit. Who wants to mount up with the wings of the greater eagle, and see beyond the curtains of time. Our eyes are not limited by what they see. Our eyes are spiritual, and see spiritual things.

The eye is the portal to the universe. I am speaking about spiritual eyes, that see the move of God, that see the glory of God, and that see the prophetic visions and dreams of the things to come.

One of my favorite prayers from Apostle Paul is when he said *"The eyes of your understanding being enlightened; that ye may know what is the hope of his calling, and what the riches of the glory of his inheritance in the saints"*.

When the eyes of the mind are Enlighted, there is a power shift in your life. You will start to experience the Word of God as the Living Word, not as a history or literature. They are any who approach the Word of God like a newspaper. David, Joshua, and Jesus magnified the Word and meditated on the Word.

Christ defeated the enemy through the Word that came through the Holy Spirit. He was a teacher of the Word, and He studied the Word. Reading nation is a winning nation, praying nation is a winning nation. Keep yourself in the love of God—dedicating your life to the will of the Holy Father against all odds.

And Joining the prayer group will strengthen your soul in trying times. Especially the prayer group where there is a frequent call to the art of fasting.

Joining a prayer group can profoundly change your life, bringing you closer to God and creating a support system that nurtures your faith. When you engage in communal prayer, you experience the power of collective faith and the encouragement of fellow believers. This shared spiritual journey can lead to personal growth, stronger relationships, and a deeper understanding of God's will for your life.

In a prayer group, you benefit from the collective wisdom and experience of others. Matthew 18:20 says, "For where two or three gather in my name, there am I with them." When you pray together, you invite God's presence into your midst uniquely and powerfully. You learn from others' experiences, share your burdens, and receive support. For instance, if you're struggling with a particular issue, someone in the group might have faced a similar situation and can offer insight and encouragement.

Furthermore, a prayer group helps keep you accountable in your spiritual journey. It can be easy to neglect personal prayer and Bible study, but meeting regularly with others provides a structured time to focus on God. Hebrews 10:24-25 encourages believers to "consider how we may spur one another on toward love and good deeds, not giving up meeting together, as some are in the habit of doing, but encouraging one another." This mutual encouragement helps you stay committed and grow in your faith.

Another significant benefit of a prayer group is the opportunity to witness answered prayers, which strengthens your faith. When you see God working in the lives of others, it reinforces your belief in His power and faithfulness. James 5:16 highlights the power of collective prayer: "Therefore confess your sins to each other and pray for each other so that you may be healed. The prayer of a righteous person is powerful and effective." Knowing that your prayers can make a tangible difference in the lives of others is deeply encouraging and motivating.

Joining a prayer group also helps you develop a sense of community and belonging. In today's fast-paced world, it's easy to feel isolated and disconnected.

9. Keep a Prayer Journal

Keeping a prayer journal as a believer who wants to walk in the Spirit and power is a transformative practice. It helps you record your prayers, track God's answers, and document dreams and visions He reveals to you. Here are some tips to guide you in this spiritual discipline, supported by scriptural insights.

A prayer journal is more than just a notebook; it is a spiritual tool that helps you deepen your relationship with God. By documenting your prayers, reflections, and spiritual experiences, you create a personal record of your walk with God. This practice encourages you to stay committed to prayer, recognize God's work in your life, and understand His guidance through dreams and visions.

How to Keep a Prayer Journal

1. **Choose the Right Journal**: Select a journal that you feel comfortable writing in. It can be a simple notebook or a more elaborate journal with prompts and sections. The key is to choose something that inspires you to write regularly.

2. **Set Aside Time Daily**: Dedicate a specific time each day for prayer journaling. This could be in the morning, evening, or any quiet time that works best for you. Consistency is crucial for making this practice a meaningful part of your spiritual routine. Psalm 5:3 says, "In the morning, Lord, you hear my voice; in the morning I lay my requests before you and wait expectantly."

3. **Start with Praise and Thanksgiving**: Begin each entry by praising God and thanking Him for His blessings. This sets a positive tone and reminds you of God's goodness. Psalm 100:4 encourages us to "Enter his gates with thanksgiving and his courts with praise; give thanks to him and praise his name."

4. **Write Your Prayers**: Document your prayers in detail. Be honest and specific about your needs, concerns, and desires. This helps you articulate your thoughts and present them clearly before God. Philippians 4:6 advises, "Do not be anxious about anything, but in every situation, by prayer and petition, with thanksgiving, present your requests to God."

5. **Record God's Answers**: Make it a habit to review your previous entries and note how God has answered your prayers. This reinforces your faith and helps you recognize His faithfulness. Psalm 77:11-12 says, "I will remember the deeds of the Lord; yes, I will remember your miracles of long ago. I will consider all your works and meditate on all your mighty deeds."

6. **Document Dreams and Visions**: Keep a section in your journal specifically for recording any dreams and visions you believe are from God. Write them down as soon as you wake up or as soon as possible, capturing every detail. Joel 2:28 promises, "And afterward, I will pour out my Spirit on all people. Your sons and daughters will prophesy, your old men will dream dreams, your young men will see visions."

7. **Reflect and Interpret**: Spend time praying over and reflecting on your dreams and visions. Ask God for

clarity and understanding. Sometimes, He may reveal their meanings immediately, while other times, understanding may come gradually. Proverbs 3:5-6 encourages us to, "Trust in the Lord with all your heart and lean not on your own understanding; in all your ways submit to him, and he will make your paths straight."

8. **Include Scripture**: Write down scriptures that resonate with your prayers, dreams, or visions. Meditating on these verses can provide insight and encouragement. Hebrews 4:12 reminds us, "For the word of God is alive and active. Sharper than any double-edged sword."

Conclusion

Keeping a prayer journal is a powerful way to walk in the Spirit and power. It helps you stay disciplined in prayer, recognize God's responses, and discern His guidance through dreams and visions. By documenting your spiritual journey, you create a personal testimony of God's faithfulness and work in your life. Embrace this practice, and let your prayer journal become a source of inspiration and growth in your relationship with God.

10. Practice Gratitude

The book of Psalms is full of gratitude. Earlier on in my Christian walk, I made a point in my life to immerse myself to the study of Psalms. My prayer language was transformed, and I started seeing the goodness of the Lord even from nature. Psalms are beautiful to start with if you want to appreciate the Lord and offer gracious praises to the Most High.

One of the men of God I studied his ministry is Father Derek Prince. In one of his writings, he says *"Psalms are the soundtracks of God"*. There were countless times when I was in serious attack from the enemy—a spiritual warfare battle won through Psalms.

Here are the best psalms of warfare; Psalms 91, Psalm 35, Psalm 27, Psalm 140, and Psalm 144. Then from 100 to 150, there are songs of praise that will inspire you to exalt the throne of God with your mouth. Your mouthpiece is the most important power force to enforce the kingdom of God on earth.

King David praised the name of the Lord at all times, in victory, in defeat, in sickness—in all seasons of life, he was redefined by the love of God. This is what he would say *"His mercy endures forever"*.

Indeed, the mercy and the love of God endure forever, whether you are in fullness, broke, sick, or healthy, know that the love and the mercy of God endures forever.

The love of God is what keeps us. The love of God was represented on the cross for all humanity to receive special deliverance.

Learn the art of gratitude. Thanks in the name of the Lord. while also upholding the laws of God. In this last age, the law of God is love in all things.

12 This is my commandment, That ye love one another, as I have loved you.

13 Greater love hath no man than this, that a man lay down his life for his friends.

14 Ye are my friends, if ye do whatsoever I command you.
John 15:12-13.

Firstly, we love God for who He is in our lives and for what He does. The love comes from the Father, shared in our hearts so that we can do the same to others. God is love. God does all things out of love. Even our faith, ought to be driven by love.

When we wake up in the morning, let us give all glory to the Lord. when we sleep, glory to the Lord. when we travel, go to malls, meetings, work etc., keep the Lord God in the name of Jesus Christ in your prayer. He shall preserve all your goings and coming in. the Lord is God. And His goodness endures forever.

The LORD shall preserve thee from all evil: he shall preserve thy soul.

8 The LORD shall preserve thy going out and thy coming in from this time forth, and even for evermore.
Psalm 121: 7-8.

Don't miss out!

Visit the website below and you can sign up to receive emails whenever Johannes Tefo publishes a new book. There's no charge and no obligation.

https://books2read.com/r/B-A-UEZX-JJKJD

BOOKS 2 READ

Connecting independent readers to independent writers.

Did you love *A Dedicated Prayer Lifestyle: Simple Tips To Effective Prayer Lifestyle*? Then you should read *Battle In The Sea: How To Tackle Spiritual Warfare And Win The Battle*[1] by Johannes Tefo!

[2]

This is a must-have book about how to tackle spiritual warfare and win in the name of the LORD. Through this profound book, you will come out armed with strategic prayers to silence the powers that have been harassing' and messing with your life. The marine kingdom is one of the deadliest kingdoms of Satan, located under the sea. This book came through a revelation. As someone who has been the victim of evil, as we all are, the

---

1. https://books2read.com/u/49aE5X

2. https://books2read.com/u/49aE5X

LORD has been gracious to me, teaching my hands how to wage the right warfare against the enemy. Through years of experience and the work of the Holy Spirit, this is the book to amplify your inner man and strengthen you in times like this. Believers have to take territory, win souls, and deliver captives, this is a must-have book filled with wisdom and knowledge for your spiritual deliverance.

Also by Johannes Tefo

Family spiritual Warfare Books
Generational Curses And Spiritual Warfare: Spiritual Strategies
& Principles Of Victory Against Evil Strongholds
Youth's Guide To Spiritual Warfare
A Women's Guide To Spiritual Warfare

Standalone
Deliver Your Soul From Evil
Overcoming Spirit Of Stagnation
The 24: Prophetic Word For This Season 2024 And Beyond
Michael For Warfare
Territorial Spirits: Overcome Evil Strongholds in Your Life And
Take Over Your Community With Strategic Warfare And Win-
ning Prayers
Prayers Against Suicide Spirit
Spiritual Warfare When Enough is Enough
Identity In Christ
Prayers Against Satanic Networks

The Workplace You Need: Spiritual Warfare Prayers That Silence Evil Powers At Your Workplace.

Deliverance From Mind Control: Be Free And Delivered From Every Marine Demons Of Mind Control

Times Getting Hard: Scriptures Of Comfort For Hard Days

Battle In The Sea: How To Tackle Spiritual Warfare And Win The Battle

Freedom: Deliverance Of Souls From Captivity

A Dedicated Prayer Lifestyle: Simple Tips To Effective Prayer Lifestyle

Redefined By Fire: Unleashing The Power Of The Holy Spirit Within.

About the Author

Before he started writing Christian books, Johannes got a graduate degree in Film and Television from university of Johannesburg. After that, just to shake things up, he went to equip himself with religious studies, particularly Christianity, just to have knack about the world beyond the curtains of time. And how this body of Christ has transformed millions of people around the world, not neglecting how sadly the movement has been persecuted from time to time. He now writes full time.